More Testimonials About

Leadership Isn't Rocket Science
6 Ways to Boost Your Leadership IQ

"This is really good, simple, yet important, information. Some people are lucky to have a good leadership mentor or boss who can teach them about leading others. Everyone else should read this book."

—Beth Brooks, CAE
President
Texas Society of Association Executives
Austin, TX

"I loved this book! *Leadership Isn't Rocket Science* is a very clever and great way to convey key leadership principles."

—Leslie Midgley, CAE
Executive Vice President
Texas Land Title Association
Austin, TX

To Chris
My fellow
book lover —
all the best

[signature]

Leadership Isn't Rocket Science
6 Ways to Boost Your Leadership IQ

Eve Becker-Doyle, CAE

★★★★
HEALTHY
≡LEARNING.™

ISBN: 978-1-60679-110-3
Library of Congress Control Number: 2010927844
Book layout: Studio J Art & Design
Cover design/photo of the Bellagio glass flower
   ceiling used as back cover border/author photo:
   Barry B. Doyle
Front cover image: © Njnightsky/Dreamstime.com
Illustrations: Barry B. Doyle; Image Club Digital Clip
   Art Collection

Healthy Learning
P.O. Box 1828
Monterey, CA 93942
www.healthylearning.com

Dedication

In memory of my dear and special friend, Bobby Gunn, the first president of the National Athletic Trainers' Association …

… and to the presidents of NATA—Denny, Kent, Julie, Chuck, and Marje—with whom it has been my honor to serve in a leadership role.

Acknowledgments

Special thanks to my wonderful spouse and life partner, Barry Doyle, whose help was invaluable, and to Emily Sawtelle. Thanks also to Chuck, Tory, Bailey, Leslie, Rachael, Mel, Colin, Beth, Mary, Gene, Marcie, Linda and the others whose affirmation and assistance have helped me in the laborious journey of *Leadership Isn't Rocket Science: 6 Ways to Boost Your Leadership IQ.*

Contents

Chapters

Appendices

Foreword

Leadership Isn't Rocket Science: 6 Ways to Boost Your Leadership IQ is a great primer for new leaders and refresher for veterans. Ms. Becker-Doyle's six tips should be standard operating procedure for leaders who want to succeed at work, at home, and in all their endeavors. I am happy Ms. Becker-Doyle has chosen to impart to you what others of us have had the good fortune to learn and model by watching her in action.

In today's world of gotcha leadership and the general inclination to promote one's own agenda before the greater good, Eve Becker-Doyle epitomizes what true leadership is about. Her style is to get things done without a personal agenda and not at someone else's expense.

With *Leadership Isn't Rocket Science: 6 Ways to Boost Your Leadership IQ*, Ms. Becker-Doyle gives us a road map to successful leadership. She suggests leading by example and common sense guidelines that bring people along together toward a shared goal. An advocate of treating people with courtesy and respect, Ms. Becker-Doyle offers methods for dealing with conflict capably but without casualties.

As a former president of the National Athletic Trainers' Association, I have worked very closely with Ms. Becker-Doyle. It has been an honor to observe, emulate, and interact with her these 10 years. I recommend you keep this helpful book handy and dog-ear the pages. My hope is that you will use these simple principles to become the best leader possible in every aspect of your life.

—Chuck Kimmel, LAT, ATC, Injury Clinic Director
Appalachian State University, Boone, NC
2004-2008 President
National Athletic Trainers' Association

Preface

In my day job as CEO of the National Athletic Trainers' Association and as a Certified Association Executive, I'm often asked to speak on what makes an effective leader. This book, which grew out of those presentations, offers simple, easy-to-remember leadership pointers.

Increase Your Leadership Smarts With These Six Tips

I contend leadership isn't rocket science. It's common sense really. Capable leaders have strong people skills, and observe the Golden Rule. People are willing to follow someone who:

- Is accessible.
- Treats people with dignity and respect.
- Gives credit and takes the blame.
- Knows when to say he or she is wrong.
- Deals with conflict when it arises.
- Listens and communicates well.

Who Should Read This Book and How Can the Questions and Cases Be Used?

Leadership Isn't Rocket Science has many applications and can be utilized in multiple contexts. With this in mind, the discussion questions have been designed to accommodate the objectives of various readers and groups. Intended to stimulate thought and discussion on the six principles, the queries:

- Can be used for individual or group leadership development and coaching.
- Apply equally well to teamwork and relationship building efforts.
- Pertain to anyone who values positive and productive interactions with others.
- Are relevant whether you are an employer, a manager, a parent, an active volunteer in your profession, PTA, homeowners club, or quilting guild … or a regular person.
- Are suitable for any aspect of working and playing well with others.

The cases are posed as leadership-related scenarios where the leader needs to take action. Essentially they are practice sessions, either individual or group, where the reader can apply what has been learned from this book.

Thanks to NATA

I wish to thank the leaders and members of the National Athletic Trainers' Association for letting me lead and serve as their chief staff executive. It is an honor to work for athletic trainers. I cannot imagine a finer group of people, or anyone who could treat me better or appreciate me more.

Best Wishes on Your Leadership Journey

My advice: Don't waste your time looking for the secrets of leadership. The best strategy is to develop your people skills.

If reading is not your thing or you're not able to complete a reading assignment for a facilitated session, don't worry. Appendix A is a cheat sheet just for you. The outline enumerates the key points for each of the six behaviors demonstrated by accomplished leaders.

Life is often simpler than it seems.

—Eve Becker-Doyle, CAE

About the Discussion Questions

The discussion questions at the end of each chapter are intended to stimulate a frank and open exchange about the leadership concepts in the book. Examining where we do and don't think alike through meaningful dialog is always a worthwhile endeavor. There is no expected outcome, and, in many cases, no single correct answer.

Requiring no advance preparation, the questions are a friend to consultants and facilitators and make group discussion easy. Groups without a facilitator will be able to navigate the questions equally well. They are effective in one-on-one coaching situations, such as a boss coaching a new supervisor or a more seasoned supervisor who needs help working with subordinates. Any individual trying to develop or sharpen leadership or people skills will find the questions of value.

The questions "From Carl's Perspective" are about Carl and his journey to effective supervision. Focusing on the story may make initial discussion easier. "From Your Perspective" queries nudge the reader to take that next step toward personal application. These draw upon the reader's individual experiences, prompting the reader to make the necessary leap from Carl's story to his or her own.

And just for fun, extra credit questions focus mostly on Mike's preoccupation with food, something I share and appreciate.

About the Case Studies

Six cases are offered for individual or group study. A leadership scenario is presented for each chapter. The assignment is to work through the leader's problem, using the ideas contained in *Leadership Isn't Rocket Science: 6 Ways to Boost Your Leadership IQ.*

Some are short case problems. The circumstances posed for Chapters 2 and 5 are more challenging. The Chapter 2 case can be done again after the epilogue, when the reader can apply the tenets learned in subsequent chapters. Chapter 5 is the most comprehensive study and necessitates some thought and consideration. To address it successfully, the reader will need to call upon most of the ideas presented in the book.

Prologue

It was Sunday night. Normally Carl was a sound sleeper, but not tonight. His body may have been lying on his bed, but his mind was racing a million miles a minute.

It wasn't a mystery why he couldn't sleep. Monday was the day of Carl's promotion and he finally became a manager. He should be getting a decent night's sleep

before starting the new job. Instead, Carl was tossing and turning, scared spitless about being a boss for the first time.

His mother had called that afternoon to wish him luck. She could tell he was on edge. In her perceptive way, she got right to the heart of the matter. "You've never been in charge of people before. How do you feel about supervising people for the first time?"

Carl had admitted this concerned him. He knew the work and had confidence in his ability to deliver what was expected from that perspective. After all, Carl had been with this company three years in another division, and he had been with another industry firm for three years before that. He knew what he was doing. That wasn't the problem.

But now that Carl had a team of his own, he needed to figure out how to lead. His mother gave pretty good advice. She thought the best way to learn something was to observe and mirror someone who did that thing well.

Tomorrow he'd start looking for the mother of all bosses to model. Having made this resolution, Carl immediately felt better. His plan was to pay attention to how other bosses bossed. In the meantime, he needed his beauty sleep if he was going to stay vertical on the job tomorrow.

Sitting in his new office and feeling a little dazed, Carl saw Mike standing in the doorway. Mike was also a manager, one of Carl's colleagues who worked on this floor. They'd met when Carl interviewed for the job.

"Hey, Carl, glad you're here!" Mike said heartily, shaking Carl's hand.

"Hi, Mike," said Carl. "It's nice to see a familiar face."

"I wanted to be among the first to welcome you," said Mike. "So, how does it feel, making your debut as a manager?"

"Great. I'm very happy to be in this new position," said Carl. "And a little scared too."

"Scared? How's that? Scared of what?" queried Mike.

"I'm nervous about bossing people. You know what I mean. I haven't supervised anyone before, so that part is new to me. I want to be an accomplished leader, and I think I've got the raw materials, but I'm not sure of the particulars," Carl continued. "I don't want to accidentally do something dumb and get off to a bad start."

"So you want to learn to boss. Clearly you didn't have a big sister," Mike commented. "Here's what I think. I always figure plagiarism is the best form of flattery—a strategy that helped me get through college. What you need is a standout role model; someone to copy."

"Funny you should say that," mused Carl. "That's just what someone told me yesterday. It sounds like a logical way to acquire some leadership smarts."

"When you hear stellar advice," asserted Mike, "you should take it. And what's more, I know someone who fits the bill."

"And who would that be?" asked Carl.

"There are plenty of folks in this building you don't want to learn the best boss curriculum from," Mike said in a low voice. "But the good news is there is a vice president down the hall who fits the bill. She's reasonable, treats her employees fairly, and gets results. In fact, she's my boss.

"If you do what Anna does, becoming a capable manager of people will be as easy as doing a paint-by-number picture. You'll be a Rembrandt in no time.

"And you'll find gaining some leadership smarts will pay off in multiple ways—not just supervising your employees. Working successfully with people in any context requires leadership skills. So whether you're a PTA officer, volunteer leader, secretary of your homeowners association, captain of your softball team, or a parent, the tips you pick up from Anna will come in handy."

"Thanks, Mike, I'll remember that," said Carl. "Sounds like Anna will be the ideal role model. I'm looking forward to making her acquaintance and seeing her in action."

And since he didn't know what else a manager was supposed to do on his first day, Carl called a meeting.

1

Be Approachable and Accessible

Rapunzel, Let Down Your Hair

By Thursday, Carl had grasped the basics of the new job. He already knew how to use the voicemail system, so that was one less thing to overload his already pushed-to-the-limit brain cells. He'd figured out where the office supplies were kept. He knew where the bathroom and the employee lunchroom were located. Arranging to have something shipped, scheduling a meeting in the conference room, and how to initiate a three-way call were all things he'd mastered. In four days, Carl was starting to get a pretty good handle on which employee was responsible for each area under his jurisdiction.

Unfortunately, Carl didn't feel he'd made any strides in learning how to be a boss. The good news was he hadn't made any flagrant mistakes yet. He attributed this turn of good fortune to the fact that it hadn't been necessary to make any significant decisions in his first days as manager. Nor had there been any staff issues that required his attention.

Although Carl had heard Anna's name a number of times as the days went by, he hadn't seen or met her. What he'd heard about the VP was positive, both from subordinates and co-workers. Anna had left for an international business trip on the day he started, and wasn't expected back for a month.

He was starting to get curious about Anna. He wondered how she'd captured the confidence and respect of the workforce. She obviously managed people successfully, so whatever she did must work. What tricks of the trade did Anna have up her sleeve? How did she do it?

About that time, Mike stopped by, raising Carl from his reverie.

"Join me for lunch?" asked Mike. "I'm starved—thought I'd head out for a hamburger."

"I'd like that," said Carl. "Red meat is good. I need to consume something manly to offset the quiche I had yesterday."

At the restaurant, Mike asked Carl about his first week as manager. "How's the new job going for you, Carl?"

"I like the work," said Carl, "and so far I have a generally positive impression of my team. I don't know everything I ought to know about management, but I'm eager to learn."

"I was fortunate when I was in your shoes," said Mike. "Soon after I moved up, Anna transferred here from another division and became my boss. She's been a good person to learn from. Watching how she interacts with her employees has been very helpful."

"Everyone seems to think Anna is a good boss, including you. Since that's one of my goals, I'm interested in hearing what makes Anna a credible supervisor," said Carl. "Can you tell me?"

Mike thought for a moment. "The first thing I noticed about Anna is she makes sure she's available to her workers. And she tends to be informal."

"What do you mean?" asked Carl.

"It's not that complicated. Anna doesn't act as if she's in an ivory tower. She's approachable and accessible to her staff and others. And the informality gives the impression she doesn't think of herself on high.

"I remember asking Anna on her first day what procedure to follow when her managers needed to see her. Did she want us to schedule an appointment with her assistant? Or did she prefer that we call or email her directly, explaining the purpose of the meeting?

"Instead, she says to me with a grin, 'When someone wants to see me, how about they just come see me?'

"Anna was saying she intended to be accessible to us when we needed her. This was a welcome change.

Anna's predecessor had been christened Rapunzel because it was so hard to get to her. Say you needed to track Rapunzel down to get the okay to go forward with a project. If you were able to, and I emphasize *if*, it was clear you were not a sight for sore eyes. You felt like you were irritating and disturbing her, and it was not a pleasant experience.

"One guy on our team frequently needed her signature on customer rush orders. Timing is critical, since the boss has to sign off before the orders can be plugged into the production schedule. He was known to lament, 'If Rapunzel doesn't let down her hair today, this customer may shear off more than my locks.'"

"I can see how that would be," said Carl, pondering. "If it seems like you're an unwelcome interruption to your boss, that would make you feel insignificant. On the other hand, having a boss who is generally approachable and accessible would give you a sense of significance and as if you make a contribution to the organization, regardless of your position."

"There's another thing about Anna that's not like the other VPs," commented Mike.

"What's that?" asked Carl.

"She doesn't allow us to screen her calls. At first we thought she was a few fries short of a Happy Meal— because that means she even takes vendor sales calls," answered Mike. "Instead of having an assistant protect her from people, Anna does the opposite, and she does it on purpose."

"I don't get it," said Carl. "Why?"

"She's trying to provide access to those who need it," Mike explained. "I guess she figures, 'So I end up with a few calls I don't need. So what?'

"Think about it," Mike went on. "When you call someone, but instead get an assistant who says, 'Ms. Brown's office,' what does that convey?"

"That the person is busy and probably doesn't want to talk to me—which gives the impression I'm not very important," Carl mused.

"And what does Anna, boss of bosses, do instead?" queried Mike. "This is your new manager pop quiz."

"Anna is not very formal and does things like taking her calls and allowing people to drop in when they need her. By making herself approachable and accessible, she ensures her employees get the answers and information to do their jobs efficiently. It also makes them feel valued and significant," replied Carl.

"Bingo! I couldn't have said it better myself. I think you're getting the hang of this, Carl." Having consumed his hamburger and fries with relish, Mike made a beeline back to the counter, where he ordered an ice cream sundae with extra fudge and whipped cream.

Discussion Questions for Chapter 1
Be Approachable and Accessible

Leaders, aspiring leaders, and just about anyone else can answer these questions and benefit from learning and thinking about the six ways to enhance leadership skills. Dialog about the concepts in *Leadership Isn't Rocket Science* will help you understand and retain the information. What you learn from reading and discussing the book should strengthen your communication skills and relationships with family, friends, and others with whom you come into contact.

From Carl's Perspective

1. What aspect of Carl's new job is causing him the greatest apprehension?
2. What strategy does Carl decide to implement for learning to boss?
3. What other strategies or ways could help someone learn constructive leadership behaviors?
4. Why did the employees of Anna's predecessor christen their boss Rapunzel?
5. What does Anna do—and not do—to enable others to have access to her?
6. What leadership lessons does Carl glean from this chapter?

From Your Perspective

7. Think back to your first experience in a supervisory position. This might be a job, such as babysitting or teaching. If you are not yet in a supervisory employment position, recall an instance when you were in charge of a volunteer project team or group school assignment, or organized a trip or event for several friends. What worried you the most? Why? How did you get through it? Would you do anything differently based on what you have read so far in *Leadership Isn't Rocket Science*?

8. Carl decided to pursue his goal of becoming a good boss by observing and studying one. Name other ways besides modeling to learn to lead effectively. What approach to acquiring leadership skills have you found most effective?

9. Why is access to a boss/leader important? How accessible are you as a boss to your subordinates? If you're not a boss, describe how accessible your boss is to you. How could that access be improved?

10. How is making others feel important and significant relevant to the workplace and in other situations involving people? Give an illustration of a situation when you were made to feel significant. Describe another in which you felt insignificant.

11. Pick one of the leadership behaviors described in this chapter and tell how it could be utilized in your work environment.

Chow Queries for Extra Credit

12. What does Carl eat for lunch when he dines out with Mike(y) Thursday?
13. With what scrumptious treat does Mike reward himself after the main course?
14. What's your favorite food?
15. Who the heck is Rapunzel and what does she have to do with the price of eggs in France?

Mini Case Problem for Chapter 1
Be Approachable and Accessible

You have accepted a post as an ESL teacher in a small school in Korea through an international relief agency. The students are of humble rural origin. Their natural cultural reticence makes it difficult for them to easily mix with outsiders. This innate shyness and the fact that you are such an oddity make you an interesting but very imposing figure to the Korean children.

You realize it will be difficult to teach the children anything until they feel comfortable interacting with you. Good thing you've just read *Leadership Isn't Rocket Science*!

Using Chapter 1 as a guide, devise a plan to de-intimidate your persona.

2

Treat People Respectfully

R-E-S-P-E-C-T! Find Out What It Means To Me

On his way to work the next day, Carl thought about his 11:00 meeting with one of his employees. What was he going to say to Ross?

This was his first chance to show his mettle as a boss. But he didn't have a clue what he should do. Should he write Ross up? Should he lecture the guy? Heck, maybe he should just kill him.

Ross had made an error ordering stock. Turns out he missed the extra zero when proofing the quantity. Ross had meant to buy 25, but when the shipment arrived, it was for 250.

While this didn't sound like a lot, it was a problem. This particular part was unusually bulky. Because quantity discounts did not apply, and Carl's area only had limited storage, the part was purposely purchased in small supply.

As Ross had pointed out, the good news was the error had no significant budgetary impact. With several months left in the fiscal year, the department would utilize the entire amount during that time without difficulty.

Now that Carl was thinking rationally, he acknowledged another thing that tipped the scale to the plus side. Ross had definitely taken ownership of his mistake. When Ross came to tell Carl about the goof, he demonstrated both initiative and tenacity by presenting a solution, as well as a plan to avert such future crises.

Still musing about his supervision dilemma, Carl headed to the company canteen for a cup of coffee. As he was stirring in some sweetener, Carl heard

the attendant tell a customer that the imprint on her teenage daughter's newest t-shirt was "SKIRTS RULE." He turned around when he heard Mike guffaw.

"Hey, Mike! I'd know that laugh anywhere. I can beat that one. My niece's favorite t-shirt says 'Hold my snowboard while I kiss your boyfriend.' My niece comes by her sass honestly, from both sides of the family."

Mike was procuring his daily caffeine fix. Evidently, a breakfast treat was on the agenda too—Mike was staring intently at the food cabinet, where the orange scones were claiming his full attention. Carl waited patiently while Mike ferreted out and ordered the largest specimen.

Then he said, "Mike, I'm having a bit of new manager anxiety, and I could use some advice."

"Hey, we're way early," responded Mike. "Want to grab a table in the back and talk a few minutes before startin' time?"

"That would be great," answered Carl. "I was really upset about this when I found out yesterday afternoon, and I made a supreme effort to keep my mouth shut. I'm not angry anymore but I have a meeting this morning with the perpetrator. I don't want to start this boss thing on the wrong foot, but I just can't decide what to say."

After they sat down, Carl outlined the situation quickly. He told Mike that Ross was not prone to error.

Mike was silent a few moments before saying, "You know, Carl, I think you're on the right track. One of the things I've learned as manager is to treat people respectfully. That's the principle you need to apply here.

"It doesn't matter whether we're talking about employees, high school kids, or the first graders I teach in Sunday school—people deserve to be treated with respect and dignity, even when they screw up.

"As I see it, Carl, you've already done two things right. First, you didn't deal with the problem when you were upset. Nobody likes being yelled at. It doesn't solve anything and only makes things worse. After you've cooled down, you regret what you've said, and how you said it. And the person on the receiving end isn't likely to find your comments enlightening or to become highly motivated to better behavior or actions by your tirade."

"Now that you lay it out that way," said Carl, "I have to agree. I had a boss at a summer job who was a yeller. He treated his dog with more respect than his employees. That didn't exactly make me want to bust my you-know-what and go the extra mile for him."

"Then you know what I mean," said Mike.

"I sure do. I wish I had less firsthand experience at being treated disrespectfully," remarked Carl. "And it's good to know I did one thing right by holding off till today to talk to Ross. So what's the second thing I didn't screw up?"

"Another way to treat people respectfully is to speak in private when there is a problem," replied Mike. "That was your second good move. Not only did you wait till you were calm to deal with this, you arranged a meeting to speak with Ross one-on-one."

"Guess I learned that on the job that summer, too," replied Carl. "My boss from hell didn't care who was around when he was in full bray. It was bad enough to have him screaming at you, but he'd do it in front of God, the warehouse crew, the office staff, and even customers.

"I vowed when I left that place I would never behave that way to an employee, my kid, or anyone. I make it a point to have sensitive or difficult conversations only in private and when I'm not annoyed. Plus I make sure I don't accuse folks. I try to ask non-offensive questions as a means of determining what's up."

"Your donkey of a boss may have been the one to hang that sign on my dry cleaner's wall," commented Mike.

"And what sign is that?" asked Carl.

Mike laughed. "The one that says, 'The beatings will stop when morale improves.'"

"That's rich," chuckled Carl. "You can be sure I didn't go back to work for the Commandant the following summer, even though he desperately needed more college kids that year, and promised me a big raise. It was a lot better pay than the place I ended up at, where I slaved and made peanuts. That was okay because the people were nice and appreciative."

"I wouldn't work for a lowlife boss like that either," said Mike. "I couldn't take a supervisor haranguing me, especially not in front of others. That would tick me off.

"A couple months ago I made a mistake here. I felt awful. I pride myself on my work, and I'm generally careful about double-checking it. This was the first time I can remember doing something so stupid," remarked Mike. "So I was having a very bad day, knowing I had to fess up to my transgression. I expected Anna to jump all over me. But when I told Anna, know what she said?"

"What?" asked Carl.

"She told me she'd get mad at me for screwing up as soon as she became perfect. I'll tell you one thing. I appreciated her treating me with courtesy and decency, and I won't forget it. When Anna asks me to jump, all I want to know is how high."

"I suppose it's a reasonable expectation that an employee would want to be treated respectfully by a supervisor," commented Carl. "And it's not hard to see why being treated that way would generate loyalty from the employee."

They checked their watches. "Are you all set?" asked Mike, brushing the crumbs from his lap as they got up from the table.

"I'm ready to rock and roll," said Carl. "Our conversation gave me an idea of how to approach Ross and what to say. Thanks for the pointers."

Discussion Questions for Chapter 2
Treat People Respectfully

From Carl's Perspective

1. When Ross's transposing error resulted in an order overage, what was Carl's initial response? What did Carl do to curtail his reaction?
2. Although Carl had strong feelings when he learned about the goof, he was impressed by how Ross handled the situation. Why?
3. What approach did Carl decide on for his 11:00 meeting with Ross?
4. How would Carl's heinous former boss have addressed the matter with Ross? Contrast that behavior with how Anna handled Mike's recent screw-up.

From Your Perspective

5. Think of an occasion when you were really POed by someone under your wing—your child, student, employee, committee member, or ____ _____. How did you get through the situation and what resolution was achieved?
6. Would you consider the encounter a success? What, if anything, might you do differently after reading this chapter?

7. Have you ever been on the receiving end of a leader's disrespectful behavior? How did you feel and react?

8. Recall an instance when your parents, boss, or committee chair reprimanded you in front of someone else. What did you take away from that experience?

9. Name one point you learned from this chapter that you hope to apply in the future.

Chow Queries for Extra Credit

10. What did Mike order for dessert, and what did he specify should be on it?

11. What did the sign at Mike's dry cleaners say?

12. If you are perfect, add 20 points.

Case Study for Chapter 2
Treat People Respectfully

You're a youth leader for your church/temple. The middle schoolers are a lot of fun and love to play jokes on each other. You're not so happy with them at this moment, however. You've just learned their latest practical joke has gone awry in a big way. A surprise decorating of the pastor's new car turned into an unfortunate incident that will require a paint job to set right.

You knew about this prank in advance and gave very specific counsel to ensure no harm was done to the vehicle. In the excitement of the moment, however, some of the kids were careless and damaged the exterior finish.

You're mad enough to 86 the lot of them. Knowing they disregarded the advice you gave to prevent this happening is particularly maddening. As youth minister, you're the stooge who gets to make explanations to the pastor. You can't wait. And you may be summoned for an explanation to the board of elders, since the incident occurred on church/temple property.

To add insult to injury, if any of the middle school kids are grounded, or barred from coming to church/temple activities for a period of time, this will jeopardize your team's chances at sweeping the Old Testament Jeopardy competition next weekend.

So count to 10 (or maybe 100). Remember, you've just read about a number of strategies relevant to this situation in *Leadership Isn't Rocket Science*. Better do some deep breathing right now. Tomorrow, when you're feeling less crazed and there's a good chance you won't throttle any car-defacing middle schoolers, have a look at the book to help you figure out what you're going to do.

You definitely need to reread Chapter 2, "Treating People Respectfully," before you talk to anyone younger than 18 about the unfortunate car decorating mishap. You'll find Appendix D, "Find Out about Screw Ups with Tact and Diplomacy," is pertinent.

If you read the whole book, use tips from at least two other chapters to help you manage this situation in a sane manner and help avoid a capital murder charge.

3

Share the Credit and Shoulder the Blame

The Devil Made Me Do It

"Hey, Gill, will you help me schlep these two boxes over to the service department?" asked Carl, as they left the customer service committee meeting. "I heard you know a shortcut."

"Happy to help," said Gill, as he hoisted one of the cartons. "And I'll show you the shortest route between the two points."

"Thanks," replied Carl, as Gill led the way down the hall toward the elevator.

"Hey, I was impressed to hear about that project your boss complimented you on in our meeting just now," said Carl. "You obviously do good work."

"Thank you," said Gill. "I like working for Mike. I've been an assistant here for quite a while, and it's been a lot nicer place to work these last several years."

"Why's that?" asked Carl.

"Anna is the catalyst. Things began to change when she came on board," remarked Gill.

"And that affected you even though she's a vice president?" asked Carl.

"Yes. And you would never know she's one of the most holy. Anna just acts like a normal person—which she is, I suppose."

"My boss has become a much better supervisor, since Anna became his boss," Gill went on, "and that's true for Anna's other managers too. Mike wasn't a bad supervisor to begin with, but we've all benefited from Anna's aura. Almost like osmosis—seems Anna rubs off on her managers even when they don't realize it. And that's a good thing."

"Yes, Mike has essentially told me that," said Carl. "He readily points out Anna is a good supervisor to model."

"Mike's on target there," agreed Gill. "The trickle down comes all the way to folks like me. Like this morning—it felt good to be acknowledged. Mike makes it a habit to share the limelight. I don't like to toot my own horn, but it's nice when the boss does, especially in front of your colleagues. He learned it by watching Anna. She is a pro at pointing out and recognizing who is responsible for successes. When Anna received a nice letter from a customer or supplier complimenting or thanking one of us, she'd read it at the next employee meeting. That was kind of cool.

"Because of our growth, that's no longer feasible. Now Anna puts the accolades in the weekly circulating file that's routed around the office. A copy of the letter goes in our personnel file and is mentioned during our performance appraisal."

"I'll bet that's pretty well received by the rank and file," remarked Carl.

"You've got that right. Last year, Anna arranged for a team member to present his cost-saving suggestion to the president. The president was impressed with the idea and immediately implemented it. Any other supervisor would have told the president herself. But Anna wanted to give her employee the exposure with the top brass and to be sure he got the credit."

"I would think Anna's workers would appreciate that. Give me an example of what Anna might say to acknowledge her employees' contributions," asked Carl.

"Anna makes it a point to recognize people specifically and personally. A couple weeks ago at a company meeting, she said something like this," Gill answered. "'Teresa, Cate, and Karen really made this project happen. I realize as VP, I get the visibility and the thank yous, but these folks did the yeoman's work and got the job done.'"

"I know from a previous job what it's like to have a supervisor who accepts praise and congratulations for the accomplishments of subordinates," remarked Carl. "Everyone resented his grandstanding. Because he was the boss, he got the perks, the business travel to great places, the expense account, and the big bucks.

Taking credit for our work was one kick in the head too many. Who needs that kind of recurrent brain injury?"

"I guess his behavior probably didn't help him gain the cooperation or good will of his employees," remarked Gill.

"Definitely not," asserted Carl, as they finally reached the service center and dropped off the boxes.

"Well, Gill, I'd better hightail it back to my department so I can plow through my email. These committee meetings are a big time gobbler."

"Here's your laugh of the day for the trip," said Gill. "Have you heard that committee meetings are like elephants mating?"

"Don't think so," said Carl. "How is that?"

Gill replied, "They're both high level, with a lot of commotion going on, and it takes two years for anything to develop."

Carl chuckled. "I'll remember that. I might need two laughs today. Got another?"

"I have a goodly number in my committee bashing repertoire," answered Gill. "Here's one more. A couple months ago Anna had the challenging privilege of chairing a committee of our VPs. In a recent staff

meeting Anna good-naturedly likened the experience to herding cats. We all got a kick out of that."

"So do I," replied Carl. "Thanks for being the trailblazer and for the animal husbandry insight, Gill. Here's my story about one of those feline VPs.

"I overheard one of them venting about the company's strategic plan not being practical or specific. His comment was, 'Our strategic plan is where the rubber meets the sky.' Insightful observation, I thought."

"Now that might be a VP who's got a brain in his head," commented Gill. "See you later."

Carl stopped by Mike's office on the way back to his own. "Do you have 10 minutes to brainstorm with me?" he asked.

"I do," replied Mike, as he finished off a Snickers® bar, "but first tell me what you think of this cool memo magnet my assistant just gave me."

Carl laughed as he read the magnet copy: 'Chocolate is the answer. Who cares what the question is?' "I have to say, Mike, that seems to suit you."

"If the shoe fits ... " grinned Mike. "Okay, what's up?"

"Back to this credit-blame thing, I think I've got the hang of the credit side of the equation," Carl explained. "But I want to know about the other part of the puzzle—'shoulder the blame.' I understand the concept; I'm not a complete idiot. But tell me more about it."

"It's not hard to figure out," answered Mike. "Another thing I learned from Anna—when something goes wrong, Anna takes the heat for any errors, because as VP, she considers it her responsibility. She depersonalizes the mistake and deflects the blame away from the individual. On the infrequent occasions when Anna refers to a departmental goof publicly or privately, she'll present it neutrally, without mention of blame.

"Of course when appropriate, Anna or I address the matter directly with the employee. But you won't find us making reference to someone's screw-up in a group."

"My vice president and I have a meeting this afternoon," explained Carl. "I've been trying to figure out how to tell him about last week's inventory ordering screw-up."

"Well, what do you think you should do?" asked Mike.

"I think I should make my boss aware of the error, but not place blame," said Carl slowly. "So I'll be careful not to say anything like, 'Ross really goofed ordering that part' or, 'Ross really screwed up.' Instead, I could say something like, 'We inadvertently overordered for that bulky part, but we've come up with both storage space and a solution for the interim. Plus, we've developed a system to avoid overages in the future.'"

"That sounds like a good plan of action," Mike remarked. "And by the way, do you have any more of that buttery popcorn? Seems like you had a box around here somewhere."

"You've come to the right place," said Carl, reaching into his desk and handing over a package. "Just don't go ape-zap as you microwave it. That burned popcorn smell puts my workers over the edge. And thanks for your help."

Driving home that evening, Carl thought, so far so good. The meeting with his boss had gone well.

He'd learned a lot about supervision, since he'd been promoted. He vowed to try to be approachable and accessible, treat his team with respect, share the credit, and shoulder the blame.

Carl slept well that night.

Discussion Questions for Chapter 3
Share the Credit and Shoulder the Blame

From Carl's Perspective

1. Anna gave very specific credit to three workers in front of their peers. Why is this important and what good outcomes result from this type of affirmation?

2. Explain the significance of Anna having an employee present his stellar idea to the president directly. Picture yourself as the employee who came up with the great cost saving idea. Envision both scenarios—one where you tell the president and one where Anna does. To what degree does each scenario make you feel affirmed, valued, and appreciated?

3. What does Mike mean when he says Anna depersonalizes a mistake?

4. Pretend you are Carl meeting with your boss the next day. What will you say to convey the ordering error?

From Your Perspective

5. How does your workplace acknowledge employees for their contributions? Could these recognition efforts be enhanced? How?

6. Recall a past boss or volunteer leader who got all the kudos by virtue of the position, and took credit for work done by you or others. Using Anna's method, remake history and come up with the right words that you wish had come out of the leader's mouth to acknowledge your contribution to a specific project.

7. How do you avoid the blaming syndrome when an employee makes a mistake, but at the same time still address the issue and make sure it's part of the personnel record?

8. What was your own mother of all mistakes at work (paying job, volunteer endeavors, or whatever)? How was this presented to others? Come up with two ways to publicly refer to what happened while deflecting blame and de-personalizing the incident. (Next time, you can draft some suggested wording for the boss, if you're not in charge.)

9. If you were/are head honcho, what new method of acknowledging employee accomplishments would you institute that would not result in any additional expense to the organization?

Chow (Mostly) Queries for Extra Credit

10. Know anyone who eats burned popcorn?
11. Or likes the smell?
12. Why is it funny to say a strategic plan is where the rubber meets the sky?

Mini Case Problem for Chapter 3
Share the Credit and
Shoulder the Blame

When you arrived late at the first meeting of the parent teacher organization at your son's school, you discovered you had been elected president. The PTO was charged to plan and put on a fundraiser. Your PTO decided to put on an auction. You have a fabulous committee that is producing what promises to be a very successful auction.

The event is tonight. While many of the auction accolades will come to you as PTO president and auction chair, you want to be sure the worker bees get the credit. What can you do tonight and in the coming weeks to see that the people who did the work are recognized for their hard work and contributions?

A beautiful vase made of expensive Murano glass was donated for the auction. Unfortunately, it shattered when your acquisitions chair dropped it this afternoon. What will you say when the donor and prospective purchasers inquire about its whereabouts tonight? Is the timing of your disclosure important?

Perfect! You just happen to have handy the outline to that great book, *Leadership Isn't Rocket Science: 6 Ways to Boost Your Leadership IQ*. Follow the points covered in Chapter 3 as you work through this exercise.

4

Apologize When You're Wrong

Love Means Never Having to Say You're Sorry ... BZZZT!

Given his newly elevated status as a manager, Carl thought he should feel better than he did. The truth was, he was not feeling exuberant. This supervisory stuff was not such a snap. If it wasn't one thing, it was another. Just when he thought he was starting to get the hang of it, another challenge would present itself.

The challenge at hand was eating crow. This was not his favorite thing, but he had to do it. His mother had taught him well. Apologize when you're wrong. If you screw-up, take ownership for your actions and say you're sorry.

Another thing she said was make sure you give a real apology. Lots of apologies aren't really apologies at all. 'I'm sorry I offended you' sounds considerably more genuine than 'I'm sorry you were offended.'

"May as well get this over with," Carl thought. "I'll feel better when it's done."

He headed for Ellie's cubicle. "Ellie, I was stricken with foot-in-mouth disease in our staff meeting today. If I could turn back the clock and undo what I said, I would. I meant to be funny, but it came out wrong, and I'm sure I embarrassed you in front of the others. At any rate, that was not my intent. I want you to know I'm sorry."

Carl and Mike met for coffee in the canteen Wednesday morning before work. Carl told Mike he'd talked with Ellie the previous afternoon.

"So you apologized to one of your employees? How did it go?" asked Mike, as he eyed the almond croissants in the display case.

"It was painful, but Ellie was gracious and seemed to appreciate the gesture," replied Carl. "I'm glad I did it. Saying you're sorry is not fun, but it's the right thing, and I feel much better now."

"I've heard Anna say," said Mike, "that apologizing when you're wrong is what a good boss does—or a good person, for that matter."

"She must know my mother," remarked Carl dryly.

"Anna thinks someone who is not big enough to recognize when he or she is wrong, and say so, does not make a good leader," added Mike. "No one wants to follow someone like that. She also says 'love means never having to say you're sorry' is horsepucky."

"My mother has a great story from when we were kids," said Carl. "The idea is if you do the wrong thing, you should make it right.

"As she tells it, at a family meeting, we agreed that any of us who exhibited certain undesirable behavior— such as hitting people—would have to wear a badge the next day as a deterrent to future misdeeds. The badges were labeled in big block letters 'I WAS MEAN', 'I WAS RUDE', and 'I SPIT.' When my mother put my little brother to bed that night, he was being a toot. She lost her temper and swatted him.

"To make it right, she paid the price for the infraction. My mother dutifully wore the 'I WAS MEAN' badge to work the next day. Naturally, that was the day the senior partner of the audit firm dropped in to review the draft audit report with her. She was pretty embarrassed to have to account for being labeled 'I WAS MEAN.'

"After that, my mom said, 'Badges? We don't need no stinkin' badges!'"

"So the stinkin' badges essentially served as a public acknowledgment and an apology for evil deeds," said Mike. "Sounds like your mom has got this stuff figured out. Maybe you got your leadership inclinations from her.

"And while I'm at it, did you ever meet someone who was constantly apologizing?" Mike went on. "Usually, it's someone with a caregiver temperament—someone who is always thinking of others and whether they are comfortable, having a nice time, and so on."

"As you describe it, a friend of mine immediately comes to mind," mused Carl. "Lisa is a caregiver. She wants everyone to be happy with everything all the time. If all is not perfect, she considers it her personal responsibility either to make it so—or at the very least, apologize for it.

"Sometimes, I've had to tell her," Carl continued, "'Lisa, I think you're the best, but if you apologize one more time for something you didn't do, I'm going to smack you.'" Carl paused, looking puzzled. "Wait a minute. Aren't we off track? What does overapologizing have to do with leading people?"

"Anna would say someone who frequently apologizes for circumstances beyond her control does not convey the image of a leader, nor does that sort of behavior inspire confidence," Mike answered.

"I guess I can see that," admitted Carl, "but it also indicates a considerate person, and what's the matter with that? Surely there's a way to be concerned about others, while still being a good leader."

"Of course," said Mike. "In this case, you approach challenges with positive thinking and humor. Anna employs this strategy often.

"If the room temperature is too cold, instead of apologizing, she'll say, 'We've purposely made this room cold to be sure you stayed awake for my enthralling report about inventory control procedures.'"

"Yes, I can see that would be a good approach," said Carl thoughtfully.

"Another time, Anna had arranged a business dinner for our group," said Mike. "Even though our reservation was for eight people, we were squeezed at a table never meant to serve that many people. But there was nothing to do for it. The restaurant was very small, it was clear no tables were turning soon, and we were on a schedule. Anna put a good face on it and said with a glint in her eye, 'I asked them to find us a smaller table, but they said this was the best they could do.'

"And by the way, that place had fabulous crème brûlée—but I digress. The point is—demonstrating humility can be the mark of a good boss and being polite is good. But being apologetic repeatedly for circumstances beyond your control does not project the confidence expected of a leader."

"Is part of your point," asked Carl, "that really nice people may have to toughen up to lead effectively?"

"Definitely!" responded Mike. "You will be a better leader if you can be less self-effacing and worry less about what other people think and feel. I realize that sounds pretty heartless, but that's how it is.

"Here's an analogy. You've heard people say that surgeons think they're God," Mike went on. "Someone with a God complex is not a person I'm going to be drawn to. But if you think about it, a sense of omnipotence is an acceptable career trait, even a desirable one, for a surgeon. How else could you cut on someone unless you have total confidence that you can fix what's wrong, rather than focus on the fact that you could kill the poor schmuck? If a doc is working on me, I'd want one who is absolutely convinced that it is completely within his or her power, along with all the king's horses and all the king's men, to put Humpty Dumpy back together again."

Carl said, "Tell me if I've got this right. You're saying in the same way surgeons must be confident to be good at what they do, leaders need to believe in themselves. This requires self confidence. And if they want to be effective, leaders can't be overly sensitive.

Am I on track here, Mike?" asked Carl, as he stood up.

"Absolutely," said Mike.

"We'd better get a move on," said Carl." Thanks for joining me for a squirt of java. I've appreciated all the good advice."

"It's as if you've done this in another life," said Mike. "In any case, you're a natural leader. You're going to be a good boss who will inspire others to follow."

Carl headed for his office, buoyed by Mike's praise. Maybe he wasn't doing so badly after all. He did a quick review of the four simple steps to supervision he'd learned so far:
1. Be approachable and accessible.
2. Treat people respectfully.
3. Share the credit and shoulder the blame.
4. Apologize when you're wrong.

As he looked at the list, Carl felt better. He was making progress.

Discussion Questions for Chapter 4
Apologize When You're Wrong

From Carl's Perspective

1. According to the mantra of Carl's mother, when you realize you've wronged someone, what should you do?
2. What did you think about the words Carl used when he talked to Ellie? Do they illustrate the leadership tips he and Mike discussed?
3. Instead of apologizing excessively for things beyond her control, what is Anna's strategy when dealing with circumstances she cannot help or control? Why?
4. What does Mike mean when he says sometimes it can be difficult for nice people to be effective leaders? What do you think about this statement?

From Your Perspective

5. Cite a specific example of a boss or volunteer leader (or colleague or parent or _____) who made a situation right by apologizing. How did you feel about this? Did it affect your opinion of him or her?
6. Share a situation where you realized you owed someone an apology. Briefly tell what happened

and what words you used. How did you feel before and after you apologized? What other consequences could have occurred had you not apologized?

7. Imagine you were facing that situation today. Think of a unique, creative and/or humorous way to say you're sorry. Do you envision the person would have responded any differently to this apology than the one you actually delivered?

8. Recall another instance—a recent one—in which you were in the dog house. What caused this and how did you extricate yourself? Would you approach the situation any differently after learning Carl's strategy?

9. Do you have a colleague or friend with a caregiver mindset? Do you fit this description? Does this have any impact on your colleague's/your friend's/your effectiveness as a leader? Explain.

10. Have you observed anyone with nice guy syndrome struggle in a leadership role? Give a specific example. What could the nice guy do to keep the syndrome from diminishing his/her performance as a leader (while still remaining a nice person)?

Chow Queries for Extra Credit

11. At the beginning of the chapter, what did Carl dread eating?

Mini Case Problem for Chapter 4
Apologize When You're Wrong

Think back to a time when you screwed up … an occasion when your actions or behavior caused problems for others that you did not intend. It may be something you felt badly about, but did not have or take the opportunity to apologize for. Or perhaps you apologized, but felt you did not adequately express your regret and concern.

Now is your chance to perfect a winsome apology, whether it's the one you never attempted or the one you wish you had delivered, instead of the words that actually fell out of your mouth. This time you can do it right, even if it's only pretend.

Try out the approaches suggested in Chapter 4 and Appendix C, "Eating Crow with Humor and Grace." They won't all be appropriate for every circumstance. Find one that fits. Or come up with a creative new way to skin the apology cat.

Who knows? You may decide to take this a step further and actually make the overdue apology. Or you could apologize again, using what you've learned, if you believe your original apology was not well done or received.

5

Acknowledge and Manage Conflict

Not for the Faint of Heart

Carl was pondering his plan of action when Mike walked in to drop off a file.

"Thanks for returning this, Mike. I hope the statistics were helpful. And as long as you're here, have you got a minute?" Carl asked. "I've got a situation…"

"This sounds like it might require some fortification," responded Mike, sitting down. "Is there any chocolate on the premises?"

Handing over a package of M&Ms®, Carl asked, "Ever heard of a book called *Between a Rock and a Hard Place*? This is an extreme example, but it's one you remember. It illustrates that taking the easy way out will get you nowhere. You've got to address the difficulty head on and do the hard thing.

"That's what this guy in the book did. He was solo hiking in Utah when his arm got pinned beneath an 800-pound boulder. Obviously, this was a big problem. Add to that the fact that this happened in a narrow slot canyon in the middle of nowhere. Five days into the ordeal, the guy figured it was do or die. So he hacks off his arm with a cheap little penknife. His one-armed self rappels 60 feet and then walks 10 miles out of the canyon to civilization, where he's evacuated by helicopter to a hospital."

"I have a special appreciation for someone who doesn't whine," said Mike. "I wish every one of my employees shared that trait.

"So does this mean you're thinking about dismembering one of your employees for some extreme infraction?"

"No, nothing like that," said Carl. "I'm going to tell a couple of my team members news they don't want to hear. I imagine they'll emerge with all their parts intact, but I feel caught between a rock and a hard place. And I don't want to take the easy way out.

"Here's the deal. I have two employees who want to be promoted to a tech position that opened up a couple days ago. I'm trying to determine the best way to manage this. I think I have it figured out. I need to speak to one, then the other, and tell them my decision. But I'd feel better getting a second opinion before I go forth and conquer."

"I'm game," said Mike, separating the red M&Ms and eating them first. "Lay it out for me, Solomon."

"The first candidate is Bonzo. His performance appraisal and project reports show that while he is more senior, clearly he's not ready for a higher-level job. He hasn't mastered the one he's in now.

"Aldo is bright and capable, but his records show he hasn't been able to maintain an attendance pattern that would allow his promotion. He's actually on probation for missing work. I hate that, because he'd be good. But clearly, I can't promote him. Even if I wanted to, our policy prohibits it.

"And there's an additional complication. I know I can't award Bonzo the promotion, given his non-stellar track record and performance. Malcolm, the manager in research and development, whom I'm told is an influential person and a relationship to cultivate, is very taken with Bonzo and favors him for the job. Last fall, during our department's slow season, Bonzo volunteered to fill in over there when an R&D worker took paternity leave. Evidently, Malcolm has had some conversations with Bonzo in which he inferred Bonzo would be in line for advancement, should an opportunity arise. I'm not keen to alienate my peer and colleague in a department we work closely with, especially in my first days on the job. But obviously, I have to do what I think is right for my department and the company."

"Lovely," remarked Mike. "So you get to talk to three people and make their day. I hope all h--- doesn't break loose. Makes me think of a magnet my mom used to keep on the fridge. It said: 'Don't make me come down there. –God.' He might need to come down here for this one."

"I hope to handle it just fine and dandy without using up my chits with the Divine Creator," Carl retorted. "I suspect I'll need His help more for year-end reviews and the news that raises may be delayed till next fiscal year if our interim financing doesn't come through."

"Good point," said Mike. "So what's the plan?"

"I've concluded the logical solution is to hire from the outside on this one," says Carl. "I wanted to treat the internal candidates fairly and ensure both were accorded the same courtesy that outside candidates will be given. So I gave them time to submit a cover letter explaining why they'd be a suitable choice, and to give me a current resume. Then I set an appointment and conducted a personal interview with each.

"Unfortunately, I didn't receive their employee files until after the interviews. If I had, I wouldn't have gone this far with either Aldo or Bonzo.

"Since I know neither is being considered, I feel I ought to say so now. I don't want to wait till we hire before telling Bonzo and Aldo. That could take weeks or months. I plan to explain why they are not candidates for this position and that we'll be hiring from outside. Why string them along when I know neither is right for this position? I should have the chutzpah to tell them."

"And Malcolm?" queried Mike. "Are you going to say something to him or do nothing?"

"I've given that some thought," pondered Carl. "I have no obligation to notify him. After all, he doesn't have jurisdiction over my area. On the other hand, I want to be smart about this. Every workplace has its share of politics and I want to be able to operate effectively in this one. I've decided I'll speak privately to Malcolm right after I've talked with Bonzo and Aldo. I won't share the particulars. I'll just give an overview and indicate I won't be filling the job internally."

"I don't want Malcolm to hear the news from someone else, especially not Bonzo," Carl went on. "I'm not going to tell Malcolm before I speak to Bonzo, since I don't wish to give the impression that Malcolm will have any input on this decision."

"That makes sense to me," said Mike. "I can't improve on your plan. Actually, I'm starting to think you're a clone of Anna, even though you've never met her. That's exactly how she'd handle this. And good luck. I'm off to manage my own menagerie."

"Thanks, Mike. I appreciate the affirmation," said Carl. "I'm going to take a few minutes to think about what I want to say and how to phrase it. I'm not always so good on my feet and usually have much better success when I don't wing it."

Carl took some time to collect his thoughts and make notes. Being fully prepared would ensure that he covered the salient points with each person and had no down time between the three meetings.

Thinking back over the day, Carl reflected on what he had learned. He was sure he had taken the right tack by notifying Bonzo and Aldo that they weren't going to be promoted. While neither was delighted with the news, both acknowledged his effort to be up front and not prolong their agony.

His conversation with Malcolm had gone well enough. Malcolm would have preferred to see Bonzo moved up, but accepted Carl's decision with relatively good grace, and thanked Carl for telling him personally.

Carl was confident he had handled three difficult conversations well and felt good about how each person responded. He hadn't been a chicken; no one could say he was lily-livered. He jotted these notes, which he entitled "Pointers for the Faint of Heart:"

1. Good leaders don't avoid conflict.
2. They address it head on but with respect.
3. Doing this promptly is important.
4. Be sure you personally convey important or unwelcome news.
5. Think in advance about desired outcomes, what to say and how to say it (because how you say things is important).

Carl thought Anna would approve of his list. He was ready to move from reflection time to Miller time. He locked his desk and headed for the parking lot.

Discussion Questions for Chapter 5
Acknowledge and Manage Conflict

From Carl's Perspective

1. What point or analogy is Carl making when he mentions the book, *Between a Rock and a Hard Place*?

2. Had you been Carl, what course of action would you have taken when Bonzo and Aldo applied for a promotion and you determined neither was suitable for advancement?

3. How did you feel about the inclusion of Malcolm in the notifications? What would you have done in Carl's shoes?

4. When Carl notifies Malcolm about Bonzo's non-promotion, Carl is engaging in office politics as a necessary evil. He would prefer not to, but Carl understands in order to be successful in the work environment he must be cognizant of political nuances and when necessary, play the game. Discuss this.

From Your Perspective

5. Recount an instance where someone in a position above you did not share bad news directly or in a timely way. How did you find out? Did how you learned about it affect how you felt

about the way things turned out? How might the unfortunate aspects of the situation have been avoided?

6. Share a situation where you were responsible for relaying unwelcome news promptly. How did this turn out? Tell what, if anything, you might do differently now.

7. As the volunteer chair of a committee, you realize you cannot renew a key committee member who is well-intentioned but has missed more than half of the meetings and simply cannot get her assignments completed. You need to replace this critical position with someone who can get the job done. Take a few minutes to plan the approach you'll take in addressing this challenge and exactly what you'll say.

Chow Queries for Extra Credit

8. What does Carl provide to fortify Mike as Mike settles in to listen and provide advice as requested?

9. Which color would you guess was Mike's favorite?

10. Which color actually tastes best?

Comprehensive Case Study
for Chapter 5
Acknowledge and Manage Conflict

Time to up the ante. You're ready now to graduate to a more extensive case study. This one will require synthesizing a number of principles and points from the book to bring this challenge to a successful resolution.

The organization you work for sponsors an annual awards competition for industry distributors. Contest winners were selected by the judges and notification letters were sent last week.

An exuberant silver winner has just called and spoken with your assistant. Your assistant passes along a message. The winner wants you to know how much she and her client appreciate your organization paying travel expenses. This is the only way they could come to accept the prestigious award in person. Without funding, they couldn't attend the ceremony. They have already bought nonrefundable plane tickets.

Your stomach lurches. Something's wrong here. You're well aware the benefits she's referring to are only offered to gold winners. A silver winner is invited to come, but at his or her own expense, and receives only a trophy.

At your request, your assistant shows you the woman's letter. It confirms the worst. The silver award letter incorrectly specified gold benefits.

Since you're the boss, you get to straighten out this mess. What on earth are you going to do?

You'll need to draw upon all your smarts and charm for this one. A good place to start is a review of Chapter 5, "Acknowledge and Address Conflict." That should provide some initial insights for dealing with this leadership challenge.

Next, see what you can garner from these parts of *Leadership Isn't Rocket Science*:
Chapter 3: Share the Credit and Shoulder the Blame
Chapter 4: Apologize When You're Wrong
Appendix E: Breaking Bad News

And don't forget these readings, especially if your assistant had something to do with the error:
Appendix D: Find Out About Screw-Ups With Tact and Diplomacy
Chapter 2: Treat People Respectfully

6

Say Things
the Right Way

Kill Foot-in-Mouth
Disease Dead!

A couple days later, around noon, Carl stopped by Mike's office. "How about we two working stiffs go to the fish and chips shop? I'll spring for it. Your advice has been right on the money, so I owe you."

Mike claimed he was always up for fine cuisine. He never missed a free meal, or any meal for that matter. Watching Mike chew rapturously on their lunch fare, Carl concluded that to Mike, all cuisine was fine cuisine. It looked like a while before Mike would come up for air.

Carl started the conversation with a one-month-on-the-job manager nugget. "In a recent spasm of lucidity, I remembered how important it is for a boss to say things the right way. Most people would agree we should pay attention to how we say what we say. But it seems to me that as a supervisor, how you phrase what you need to get across becomes even more critical.

"This was evident when I spoke to Bonzo and Aldo," Carl continued. "I spent time thinking about the best way to tell them the promotion was a no-go.

"It really helped me," Carl said. "For one thing, I felt more confident since I wasn't blundering about searching for the right words and approach. My notes were helpful and kept me on track. Plus, the notes function as a record of my conversations for the personnel file. And another thing—this may sound silly, but having notes shows the employee you think the encounter is important and you value him or her enough to have spent time planning for your meeting."

Having stuffed a big bite of fish into his mouth, Mike responded with an affirmative-sounding grunt. Carl took this to be agreement, noting the vigorous head nodding that accompanied the grunting.

"We talked before about apologizing when you're wrong," Carl went on. "How you say you're sorry is important. After our conversation, I began compiling a list of apologies for future use. Any preventative effort to keep me out of the doghouse is worthwhile."

Having plowed his way around to the outside of his plate, Mike was now eyeing Carl's uneaten chips. "I agree the wording of an apology is important," Mike said. "Anyone who's married knows that.

"Looks like you've only been grazing," Mike commented. "Got anything there you're not planning to consume?"

Carl handed over the chips, saying, "It definitely applies to treating our employees respectfully. Remember Ross's inventory ordering mistake? I needed to talk to him about what happened and what to do about it.

"The questions that were coming to mind when I was hopping mad were accusatory. My first inclination was to ask, 'How on earth did this happen?' or 'What were you thinking?' or 'Are you brain dead?' The least offensive one I was able to come up with was 'Tell me about the screw-up.'

"I don't think with that approach we could have had a productive conversation. When we met the next day," Carl remarked, "you and I had talked, and I'd had a chance to think about it. It was clear to me that I should take a more neutral, get-the-information approach, which would allow for the possibility that there were contributing factors I was not aware of, would be more respectful, and would not put Ross on the defensive."

"So, I came at it from the standpoint of 'Tell me about the order we received this morning.' I tried to keep my follow-up questions neutral as well. 'Why was that?' 'How did that come to pass?' and 'What are your thoughts about how to deal with the extra inventory?'"

Having made short order of the fries, Mike downed the rest of his Dr. Pepper®. "That makes sense," Mike said. "Why do I think now you're going to tell me that saying things the right way applies to sharing the credit and taking the blame too?"

"Matter of fact, I am," admitted Carl. "That's an area where phraseology is definitely relevant.

"Here are two ways to give credit when it's due," said Carl. "I could say, 'Thanks to team two for producing this resource' or I could say this: 'I'd like to congratulate team two for its outstanding work developing the new resource. Would you all please stand? I especially wish to recognize Ashley. Without her hard work, coordination, and follow-up, this project would not have happened. Justin and Rachael were essential parts of this winning equation as well, and were strong contributors to the process. My thanks to you all.'"

Mike remarked, "It's obvious your second statement reflects more thought and effort and gives specific, personal recognition. Of course, the employees will feel more affirmed and valued by those words. It easily trumps your first brief, generic sentence."

"That brings us to shouldering the blame," Carl said. "In some situations, it may not be appropriate for the boss to actually take responsibility for the mistake, but you can de-emphasize the error by using humor and being positive.

"Here's an example. At a department meeting, your assistant hands out the photocopies you asked her to make. You notice the pages are upside down and out of order.

"You don't ignore the error, nor do you focus on it. Since it's obvious, you acknowledge it.

"You might say, 'The photocopy gremlins have been stirring up trouble and copied this document all catty wampus. Pay them no mind.' Or you might say, 'As you see, the little man inside the copier was feeling obstreperous today and refused to cooperate. Reminds me of my kids.'"

"And if it's a matter of significance, you address the issue later one-on-one with the employee," added Mike.

"Right," said Carl. "By the way, in the course of our ongoing chats about how to be a good boss, I've had an epiphany."

"I await this astounding revelation with great impatience," quipped Mike. "Let's hear this pearl of wisdom."

"Here it is: Good communication goes hand in hand with good leadership," Carl expounded. "My amazing insight brings to mind a great turn of phrase. Maya Angelou proclaimed that her grandmother, an excellent cook, 'knew how to sling groceries together,'" Carl said. "In the same way, I've realized my effectiveness as a manager has a direct correlation to how well I sling the words together as I apply those leadership behaviors.

"Put another way, the leadership tips you've given me work best, if, as I implement them, I select the right words and tone to convey my messages."

"No one's going to disagree with your point that communication is essential to being a good manager," commented Mike. "Lucky for you, Carl, you're a pretty decent communicator, so there may be hope for you yet.

"Now that I think about it," Mike said, "while I don't think I've ever put a name to it like you have—Anna does all of these things. She considers her words and chooses them carefully. She definitely makes an effort to say things the right way in all her dealings with employees and colleagues."

"Why does that not surprise me?" remarked Carl.

On the way back to the office, Mike told Carl, "Hey, while the juices are flowing, you ought to expand that list of apologies into a more comprehensive list. You could include other work scenarios too, like breaking bad news, or asking about problem situations without putting your employees on the defensive.

"Then, when you find yourself afflicted with say-it-right block, you can pull out the silver-tongued remarks you prepared in a moment of inspiration."

"Good idea," said Carl. And when he got back to the office, that's what he did.

Discussion Questions for Chapter 6
Say Things the Right Way

From Carl's Perspective

1. Carl seems to gain supervisory confidence as time goes on. Recount instances from the story that demonstrate this. Is this a natural progression?
2. Explain how saying things the right way applies to all the principles Carl and Mike talk about in this book. Give examples of how to say something the right way and the wrong way for two of the leadership principles.
3. Add three new ways to say you're sorry to Carl's list.
4. Why do Carl and Anna think humor is an important component in communicating to those you lead?

From Your Perspective

5. Did your boss, teacher, or parent ever misread a situation and judge you guilty when you were not at fault? What did he or she do and say?
6. How did the leader's reaction make you feel? What could the leader have said or asked instead that could have prevented the misunderstanding?
7. Describe an instance when you had to determine the specifics of an employee's (or student's,

child's, ...) error. How did you go about eliciting the information? Did you discover anything you were not initially aware of?

8. What would you do differently now, based on what you've read in this chapter?

Chow Queries for Extra Credit

9. What sentiment does Mike's grunt convey?
10. What are chips?
11. Who likes free food?

Mini Case Problem for Chapter 6
Say Things the Right Way

You are treasurer of your local Toastmasters club. Last year, your hard work was recognized when you received the district's Outstanding Toastmasters Club Treasurer award.

For the third time, you've been asked to lead a weekend workshop to train new club treasurers from your district. You enjoy training and developing others and are happy to contribute in this way. Presenting the half-day session, however, involves considerable preparation, a 45-minute drive to and from the venue, and takes the better part of your Saturday.

When you arrive, the woman at the registration desk asks you to pay the event registration fee. This is a first. You explain you are not attending the day of education, but are simply presenting at one of the morning sessions.

She looks perplexed. She appeals to the top officer for the region, who is walking by the desk. He confirms that everyone, regardless of function or purpose, pays the $10.

You're steamed. Making a volunteer feel unappreciated is a bad strategy for retaining volunteers. You pay the money, but this workshop will be the last time you give up your day off to drive to Timbuktu-land to train treasurers for Toastmasters.

Let's assume it was necessary to assess the $10 fee to all, speaker or attendee. Use some of the approaches suggested in Chapter 6, "Say Things the Right Way," to come up with a positive, upbeat way to explain the new policy. Can you think of other measures that could have been taken to make the situation more palatable or to clarify in advance the expectation that speakers and attendees pay entrance fees?

Epilogue

Monday morning, after a month on the job, Carl was at his desk. A woman tapped on his open door and stepped in. "Hi, Carl. I'm Anna. Glad to meet you. I've been on the road for a while."

"Hey, Anna!" exclaimed Carl. "I've been looking forward to meeting you. How was your trip?"

"Mainly it was long," said Anna. "But I accomplished everything I planned to, so I was pleased. It's good to be back on the home front.

"Now that you have a few weeks under your belt as a manager, tell me how things are going."

"Pretty well," answered Carl. "I've been trying to learn to boss. The leading people part is important and I want to do it right."

"You know, Carl, supervision isn't rocket science. It's pretty simple," said Anna. "Being a good boss is just doing what a good person does and treating people right. There's not really a whole lot more to it."

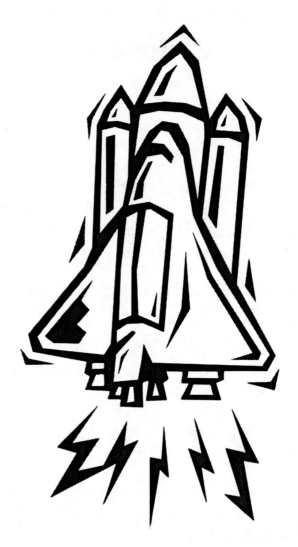

"I guess treating people right is a good summary statement for what makes a good manager. At first, I thought supervising and leadership were more mysterious than that. But these six steps aren't hard." Carl ticked them off on his fingers:

- Be approachable and accessible.
- Treat people respectfully
- Share the credit and shoulder the blame.
- Apologize when you're wrong.
- Acknowledge and manage conflict.
- Say things the right way.

"That about sums it up," said Anna, looking surprised. "Sounds like you know all my secrets."

"That's right. From all I've heard, I know this stuff works for you," claimed Carl. "So I have every intention of doing what you do."

With a straight face, Anna said, "Smart kid." Then she grinned, "Welcome aboard."

A

Cheat Sheet of Carl's (Newly Acquired) Leadership Insights

Outline for
Leadership Isn't Rocket Science
6 Ways to Boost Your Leadership IQ

1. Be approachable and accessible.

- Act informally and help people feel at ease.
- Allow people to drop in when possible.
- Don't screen your calls.
- Make people feel significant.
- Provide your employees the information and answers they need to do their jobs.

2. Treat people respectfully.

- Wait until you're calm.
- Figure out and comment on what was done right.
- Expressing anger toward others is disrespectful and unproductive.
- Speak in private about problems.
- When deciding how to handle a situation, consider how you'd like to be treated if circumstances were reversed.
- Remember, no one's perfect.

3. Share the credit and shoulder the blame.

- Compliment employees for their successes.
- Recognize them publicly—to peers and bosses—for their accomplishments.

- Give acclaim to those who did the work when you receive the kudos.
- Be specific and personal when giving credit.
- Take the heat for errors of subordinates.
- Acknowledge but depersonalize mistakes in public situations when necessary, but address them privately.
- Avoid and deflect blame.

4. Apologize when you're wrong.

- Take ownership for your actions.
- Recognize when you're wrong and say so.
- Make sure an apology is truly an apology.
- Don't overapologize or apologize for things beyond your control (for example, the weather).
- Instead, use positive thinking and humor.
- Nice people may need to get tough to lead well.

5. Acknowledge and address conflict.

- Face up to and do the hard stuff.
- Do so in a timely manner.
- Convey important or unwelcome news personally.
- Think in advance about desired outcomes.
- Spend time preparing what you want to say.

6. Say things the right way.

- Carefully consider language and tone, which affect how people hear and respond to your message.
- Avoid stating assumptions or accusations, since there are probably things you don't know.
- Instead, ask neutral questions when there's a problem and follow up with more non-accusatory questions.
- Craft messages with deliberation and care, especially for anything sensitive.
- Good communication skills are essential for leaders.
- Model experienced communicators who use language, humor, and tone well.

B

Cheat Sheet
of the Players

The Cast of Characters

Main Characters

Carl   The newbie, recently promoted to
                    manager

Anna   Vice president on the same floor;
                    example of a good boss; away for four
                    weeks on an international business
                    trip

Mike   Manager just down the hall; Carl's
                    peer who works for Anna; likes his
                    chow

Cameo Appearance

Ross   Carl's employee who orders way too
                    many bulky parts

Gill   Longtime assistant who works for
                    Mike; knows his way around

Non-Cameo Appearance

Ellie   Employee to whom Carl delivers an
                    apology

Lisa   Carl's friend who apologizes for things
                    that are not her fault

Just an Honorable Mention

Mom   Carl's mother, fabulous woman, says no more stinkin' badges

Nameless   Carl's boss, a vice president

Maya Angelou   Celebrated African American author, poet, film director, television producer, actress, journalist, educator, activist, dancer; recited her poem "On the Pulse of Morning" at Bill Clinton's 1993 inauguration

Hardly Worth Mentioning

Nameless   Carl's heinous former boss; yells a lot; treats his animals better than his employees

C

Eating Crow With Humor and Grace

Apologies

- I can't believe I ___. What a dope! Please forgive me.
- I regret doing/saying ___. I wasn't thinking. I'm so sorry.
- I didn't intend to ___. Please accept my apologies.
- I didn't realize ___. I feel badly and want you to know how sorry I am.
- My face is red! I've really done it this time. Please forgive me.
- I'm a total goof. I had no idea ___. I'm really sorry.
- What can I say except that I'm a total idiot? I feel awful about it. I'm so sorry.
- I get the dolt (goof up, idiot, jerk, you fill in the blank) of the year award. Please forgive me.
- I don't try to act like a jerk. It just comes naturally. Please forgive me.
- I'm not an idiot intentionally. I'm just completely clueless. Please accept my apology.
- I'm not an insensitive jerk on purpose. It's genetic. How can I make it up to you?

Accepting an Apology
(Graciously)

- I appreciate you saying that. Please think no more about it.
- I accept your apology. Let us speak no more of it/the matter.
- Thank you. It's behind us now, and we'll go forward from here.
- Not a problem. We can work this out.
- It happens. I appreciate you saying that, but please, let's forget it.
- It's ok. I've done the very same thing. In fact, one time I ...
- I do things like that all the time. Don't worry about it.
- Thank you for the apology. Let's put it behind us.

D

Find Out About
Screw-Ups With
Tact and Diplomacy

Find Out About
Mistakes or Problems

- How did this come to pass?
- Tell me about it/the situation.
- What caused this chain of events?

Obtain More Information

- And then what happened?
- Why was that?
- How is that?
- What are your thoughts about how to deal with this situation?
- What could you do differently to avoid this scenario in the future/prevent this from happening again?
- How can we set it right?
- What would you suggest at this point?

Breaking Bad News

In Chapter 5, "Acknowledge and Manage Conflict," Carl told two employees they were unsuccessful in their venture for a promotion. Wanting to be sure he phrased things properly, Carl took time thinking about what to say and made notes.

* * *

What Carl Said to Bonzo and the Subsequent Exchange

"Bonzo, I want to be up front with you. After evaluating your application and your file, I can see you're not where you need to be to be considered for promotion. I'm sorry this is not the answer you're hoping for, but it shouldn't be a surprise either. Your performance appraisals pinpoint several areas requiring improvement.

"In reviewing your project reports, I can see while there is some movement in the right direction, you have not yet achieved the level of competency required in your position. If you're not fully successful in your job now, it would be a disservice to you and the company to move you into a higher level one."

"I know that I haven't achieved all of my goals and performance measures, but I thought since I'd been here nine years, I'd have a good chance," said Bonzo.

"Can I be considered for promotion at some time in the future?"

"Bonzo, I understand your desire to know what you can expect. Unfortunately, there's no way for me to say. I can't give you an answer because I don't know what factors we may be dealing with in the future or what circumstances may arise," Carl remarked. "This much is clear. Before such a thing could even be a possibility, you'd need to be performing beyond basic competency in your current job. You should be excelling at what you're doing before it's realistic even to discuss a promotion."

"I'm disappointed but I see what you're saying. I appreciate that you have been straight with me," replied Bonzo. "At least you didn't keep me hanging while you interview from the outside. That would have been worse. My last manager wasn't very direct and didn't like dealing with this kind of stuff, so I never really knew where I stood. At review time, she was required to talk to me about performance, but that was the only time she ever gave any feedback, good or bad. I may not like what you're saying, but I prefer to know what you're thinking and where I stand."

"Sounds like you're talking about the manager I've heard referred to as Rapunzel," said Carl.

"One and the same," answered Bonzo.

* * *

Carl figured the encounter could have been worse. Bonzo didn't go postal; he seemed to take it pretty well.

What Carl Told Aldo and How Aldo Responded

"Aldo, I need to follow up about the vacant position. I won't subject you to a lot of preamble, so I'll get to the point. I regret we can't consider you for promotion. While I believe you have the capability to make a good level two technician, you are on probation due to excessive absences.

"That's a problem for at least two reasons. First of all, our employee handbook stipulates workers on probation are not eligible for any movement within the company. That applies to both promotion and lateral transfer. Second, it is vital that the level two technician be here every day to cover the phones. Frankly, your current attendance profile does not offer any assurances that would happen."

With a forlorn, hang dog expression, Aldo said, "I was hoping you could overlook my time out of the office, but I realize what you're saying is true. I won't buck you on this one; I understand. I hope to get my personal circumstances straightened out, so I can lick this problem long before the next promotion opportunity surfaces. And thanks for telling me now. It would have been difficult to have this drag on and on. That was the style of our previous boss; maybe you've heard of Rapunzel. She was the queen of nondisclosure."

Aldo told him Rapunzel had been notorious for avoiding conflict, staying out of sight, especially when it was time to convey bad news to the rank and file. "We always knew she'd keep to the tower if anything unpleasant needed doing. More than once, this resulted in employees finding out from people in other departments or colleagues what they should have been advised by the boss.

"It was hard to respect someone like that," Aldo said. "Seems like at the very least a boss's job is to advise us plebes what's going on—whether it's a policy change, new attendance rules, or that my promotion is a no go.

"One of my friends found out he was slated to move to another department by reading about it in the company newsletter. Here's how another woman discovered she wasn't getting a raise: Human resources told her the bad news when she asked them why her paycheck hadn't gone up."

Carl had to agree with Aldo. When bosses refused to boss and do the hard things, the result was resentful employees and poor morale.

As soon as Aldo left, Carl headed for Malcolm's office. May as well go for the hat trick and knock out the third of today's unpleasant encounters, he thought.

About the Author

As CEO of the 40-employee National Athletic Trainers' Association, a former personnel director, and an active volunteer in association executive and other nonprofit groups, Eve Becker-Doyle has had plenty of leadership experience.

Becker-Doyle doesn't claim to be a leadership guru. She readily admits while she gets a lot of her supervision, management, and leadership responsibilities right, she messes up too. When something goes wrong, Becker-Doyle often finds she's strayed from or neglected to utilize the six principles outlined in this book. Gleaned from Becker-Doyle's leadership journey, the precepts offer leaders and aspiring leaders a common sense approach to leading, supervising, and managing others.

A Certified Association Executive, Becker-Doyle has served on the American Society of Association Executives board and chaired its Human Resources Committee and Political Action Committee, as well as its Finance and Administration Section and Executive Management Section councils. She led a work group that developed ASAE's on-line CEO Excellence curriculum.

Both the state and local association executive groups have honored Becker-Doyle with their premier award for her contributions. In 2001, she was named the Texas Society of Association Executives Distinguished Executive. The Dallas Fort Worth Society of Association Executives presented her with its Excellence Award in 1999.

Becker-Doyle speaks on the characteristics and behaviors of effective leaders; hiring, evaluating, and retaining employees; strategies for dealing with leadership snafus, and related topics.

Becker-Doyle's affiliation by marriage to professional photographer Barry B. Doyle has produced three curious offspring. All are happily straining the family budget with college housing and tuition bills.

Order Information

Leadership Isn't Rocket Science
6 Ways to Boost Your Leadership IQ
Eve Becker-Doyle, CAE
$14.95 • 978-1-60679-110-3

Additional copies of
Leadership Isn't Rocket Science
6 Ways to Boost Your Leadership IQ
may be ordered in four ways:

Online: www.healthylearning.com

Phone: 888.229.5745

Fax: 831.372.6075

Mail: P.O. Box 1828
Monterey, CA 93942